Smithsonian kids

DINOSAURS
GUIDEBOOK & PROJECTOR

Silver Dolphin

What Are Dinosaurs?

Dinosaurs. Our imagination runs wild just at the sound of that word. Gigantic prehistoric creatures with weapons for body parts—it just doesn't get any more exciting than that. Of course, when we stop to think about it, we know dinosaurs weren't all gigantic, and they weren't all deadly. It's just fun to scare ourselves in the safety of our bedrooms.

Dinosaurs first appeared on Earth over 233 million years ago. It's hard to imagine just how long ago that really was. But we can imagine what the world might have been like with no people or buildings.

DISK 1 1 See *Ankylosaurus* on Disk 1, Slide 1.

For more than 165 million years, dinosaurs continued to stomp around, diversifying in size and number. But they weren't the only prehistoric creatures. Life on Earth began over 3.6 billion years ago in the ocean and eventually made its way onto land. Plants, insects, reptiles, amphibians, and a host of other animals were already on Earth by the time dinosaurs arrived.

300-200 MILLION YEARS AGO

Before humans inhabited Earth, the planet was much different than it is today. All of the land on Earth was crunched into a giant continent called Pangaea. When dinosaurs emerged, around 233 million years ago, the land was hot and dry.

Around 200 million years ago, the planet was warmer than today. Pangaea started to break up into the northern supercontinent Laurasia and the southern supercontinent of Gondwana, later creating the landmasses and bodies of water we know today.

Most everything we know about dinosaurs comes from parts of their bodies, their footprints, burrows, and dung preserved as fossils. Because people are always finding new fossils and making new discoveries, what we know about dinosaurs is constantly expanding.

2 See a fossil on Slide 2.

Dinosaur footprint fossil

The Age of Dinosaurs

Dinosaurs lived during the Mesozoic Era, which is divided into three periods: Triassic, Jurassic, and Cretaceous.

The Triassic period was 252-201 million years ago, the Jurassic period was 201-145 million years ago, and the Cretaceous period was 145-66 million years ago. We know something catastrophic happened to kill off the dinosaurs, but that wasn't the first time something like that occurred. At the start of the Triassic period, 252 million years ago, 90-96 percent of the world's species were wiped off Earth on both the land and in the sea. During the first several million years of the Triassic period, life struggled to recover. Eventually new species of plants and animals evolved around the globe. Dinosaurs were among those that evolved during the middle Triassic.

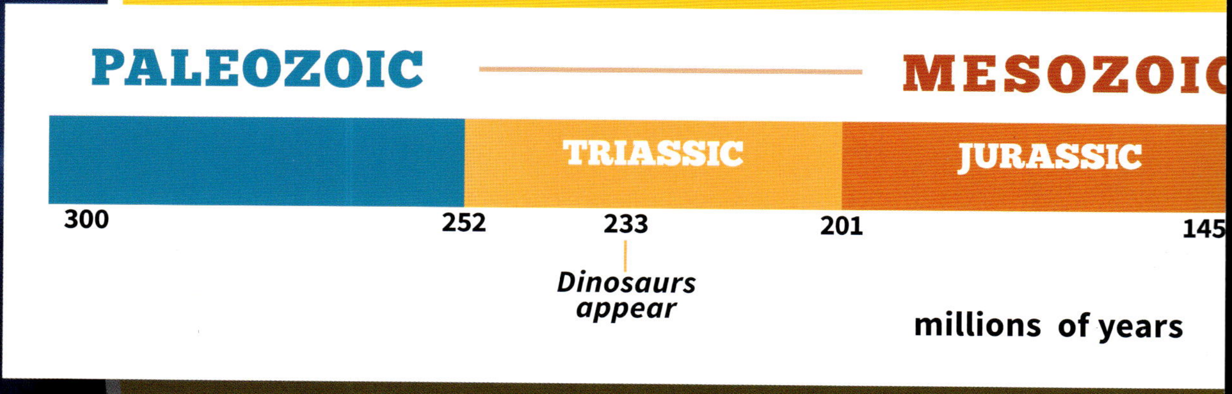

3 See an early mammal, *Juramaia,* on Slide 3.

Triassic Period

At the start of the Triassic period, all of the continents we know today were connected as the supercontinent Pangaea. Toward the end of the Triassic period, small to medium-sized dinosaurs emerged followed by the first true mammals.

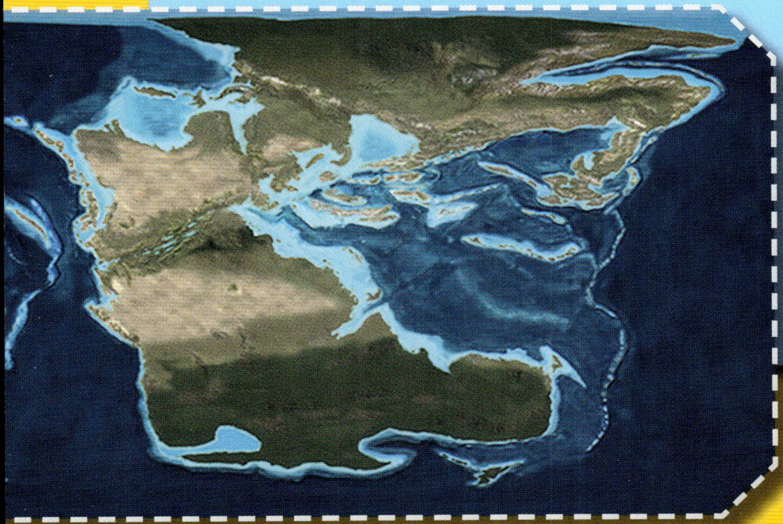

The world was generally warmer and drier than it is today, and Pangaea was beginning to split apart.

ERA — CENOZOIC

CRETACEOUS

66 present

Jurassic Period

During the Jurassic period, Earth was generally warmer and wetter than it is today, and the land was covered in trees, ferns, and other greenery. Some of the biggest and most recognizable dinosaurs, including the sauropods, lived during this period.

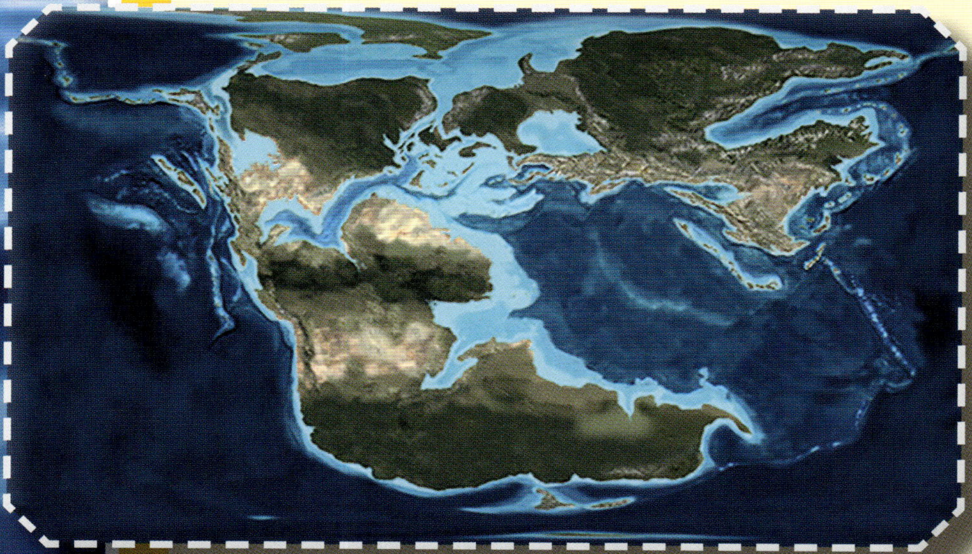

4 See *Diplodocus* on Slide 4.

Cretaceous Period

Dinosaurs continued to thrive and new dinosaurs were coming into being during the Cretaceous period. Paleontologists have found fossils for the first true birds and flowering plants from this time period. Pangaea continued to break apart, and extinction of all the dinosaurs except birds occurred.

DISK 2
1
See *Dakotaraptor* on Disk 2, Slide 1.

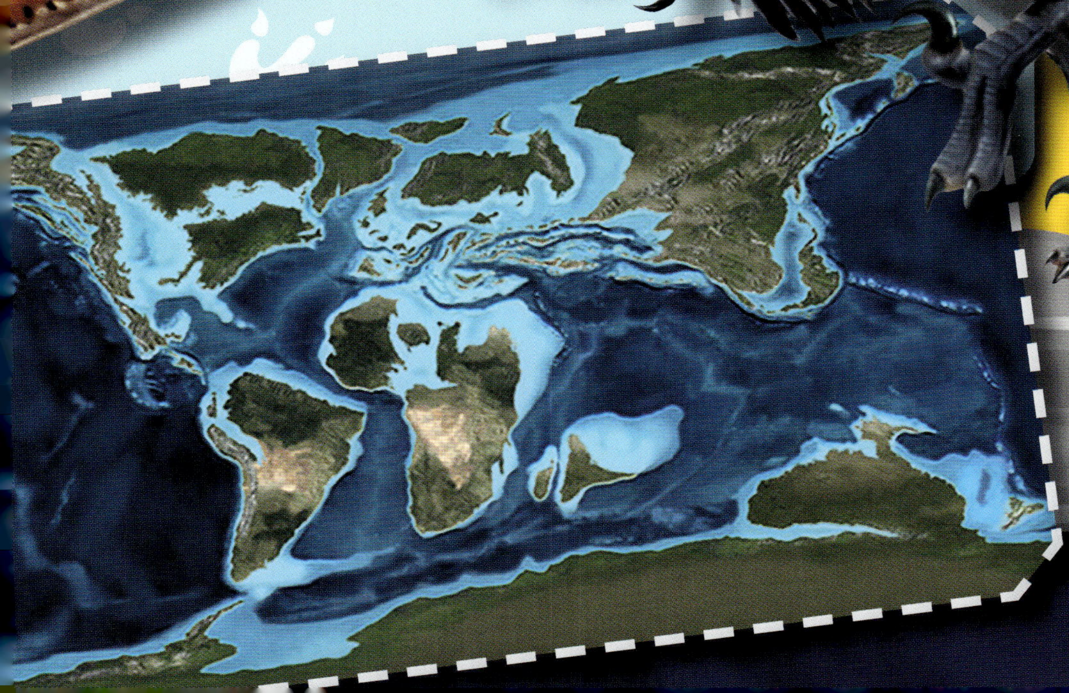

Triassic Dinosaurs

2 See *Eoraptor* on Slide 2.

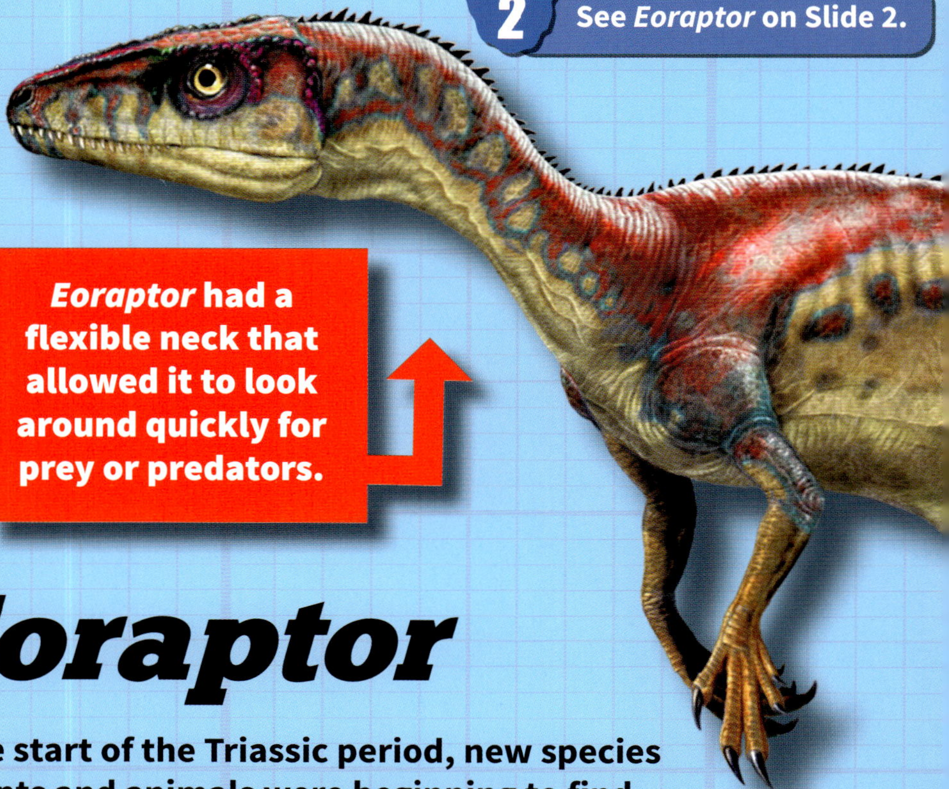

***Eoraptor* had a flexible neck that allowed it to look around quickly for prey or predators.**

Eoraptor

By the start of the Triassic period, new species of plants and animals were beginning to find their place on Earth. *Eoraptor* was a small, speedy dinosaur that lived in what is now present-day Argentina. Its name means "dawn thief" because it lived during the dawn or beginning of the age of dinosaurs. In 1991, an *Eoraptor* was discovered in Argentina's Valley of the Moon by paleontologists Fernando Novas and Paul Sereno.

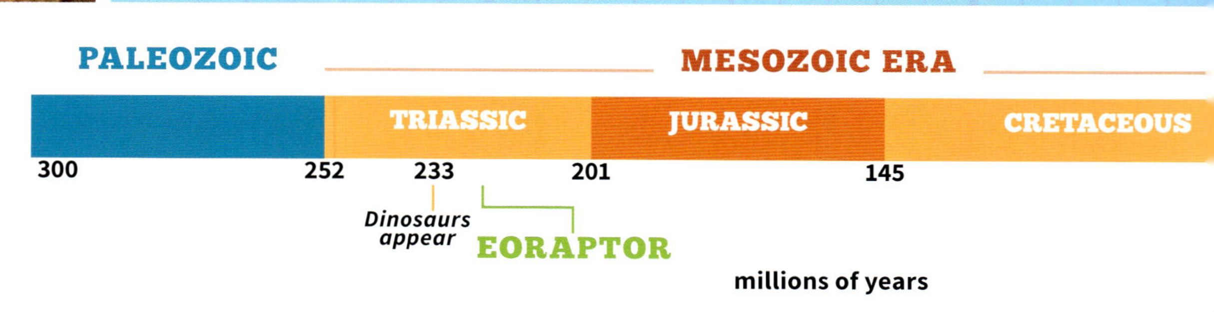

Eoraptor

Name Meaning: Dawn thief
Size: 3 feet long; 22 pounds
Diet: Animals
Fossils Found In: Argentina

Did You Know?

When scientists first studied *Eoraptor's* teeth, they thought it only ate meat. But a closer look at the front teeth revealed broader teeth suited for eating plants. Now scientists believe *Eoraptor* ate both plants and meat.

A long tail helped *Eoraptor* balance while it ran.

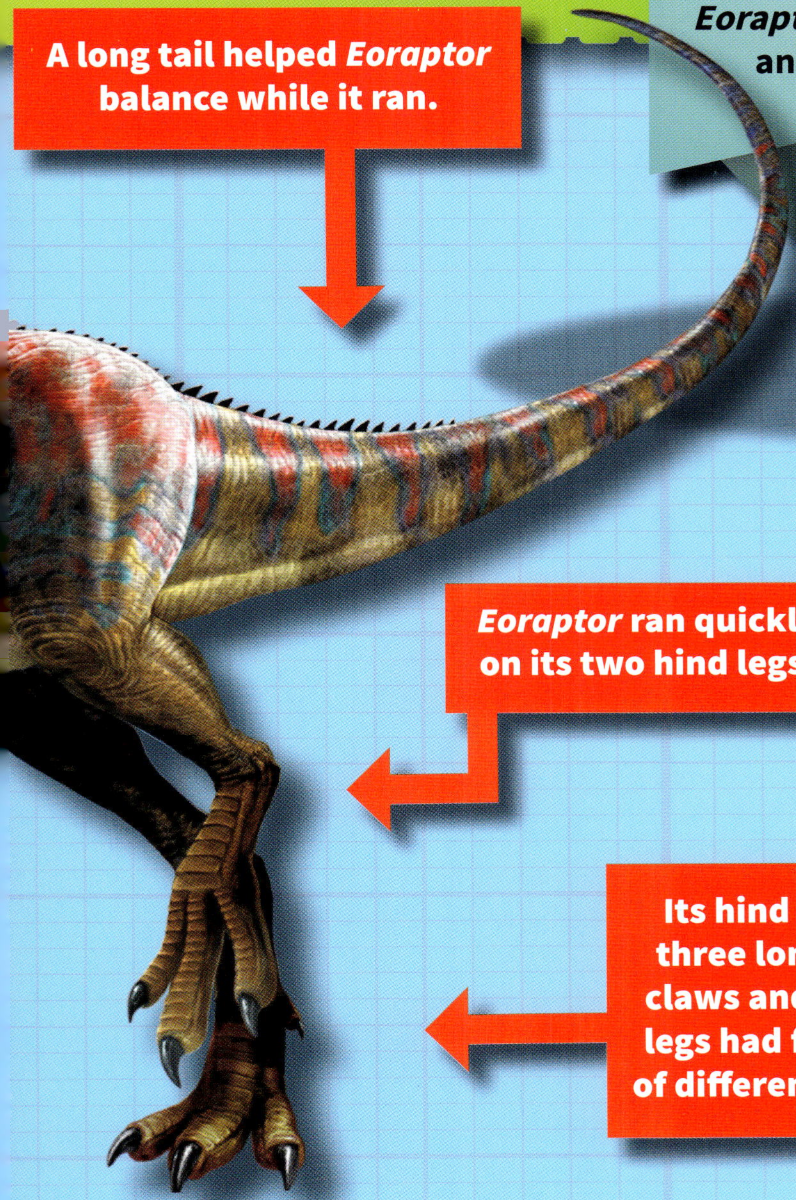

Eoraptor ran quickly on its two hind legs.

Its hind legs had three long, sharp claws and its front legs had five claws of different lengths.

CENOZOIC

66 present

Triassic Dinosaurs

The lower jaw contained sharp teeth that curved inward, which helped *Herrerasaurus* grip prey.

Three curved claws helped *Herrerasaurus* grasp and rake.

Herrerasaurus

Herrerasaurus fossils were discovered in the same place as *Eoraptor*—Argentina's Valley of the Moon. The first incomplete skeleton was uncovered in 1958 by a farmer named Victorino Herrera, whom the dinosaur is named after. In 1988, paleontologist Paul Sereno discovered a complete skull. Paired with the earlier findings, scientists successfully reconstructed the *Herrerasaurus*.

Herrerasaurus

Name Meaning: Herrera's lizard
Size: 13 feet long; 463 pounds
Diet: Animals
Fossils Found In: Argentina

Did You Know?

Although *Herrerasaurus* was a predator, it was still probably killed and eaten by bigger predatory reptiles more closely related to crocodilians, called rauisuchids.

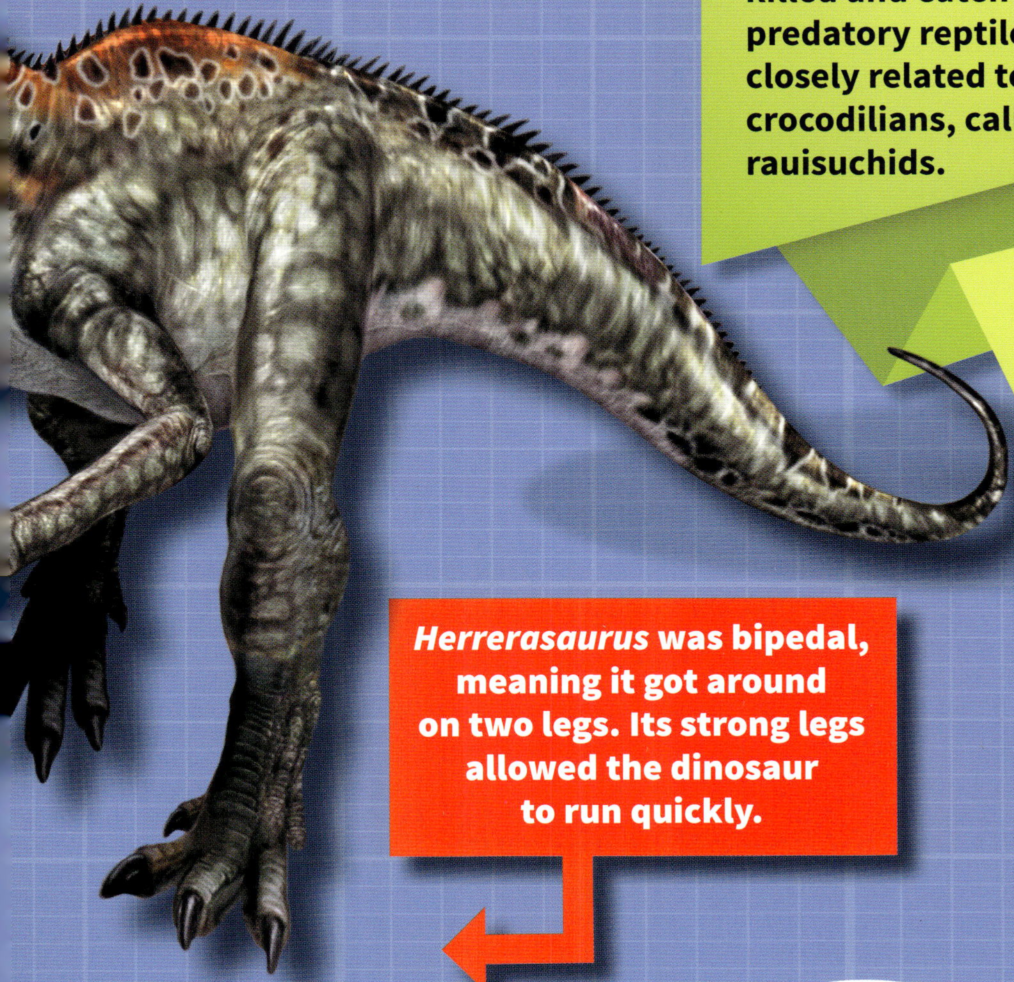

Herrerasaurus was bipedal, meaning it got around on two legs. Its strong legs allowed the dinosaur to run quickly.

3 See *Herrerasaurus* on Slide 3.

CENOZOIC
66 present

FAST FACT

Herrerasaurus was about as long as a small car.

Jurassic Dinosaurs

Brachiosaurus

The largest dinosaurs to roam Earth didn't eat other animals—they ate plants! *Brachiosaurus* had to eat more than 400 pounds of food every day just to survive. More than twice as tall as a giraffe, *Brachiosaurus* was a true giant! Its long neck allowed it to eat leaves from the highest branches of trees.

Due to their sheer size, sauropods are extremely difficult to dig up. It took hundreds of workers three years of diligent work to unearth the first *Brachiosaurus* skeleton, which was found in western Colorado in 1900.

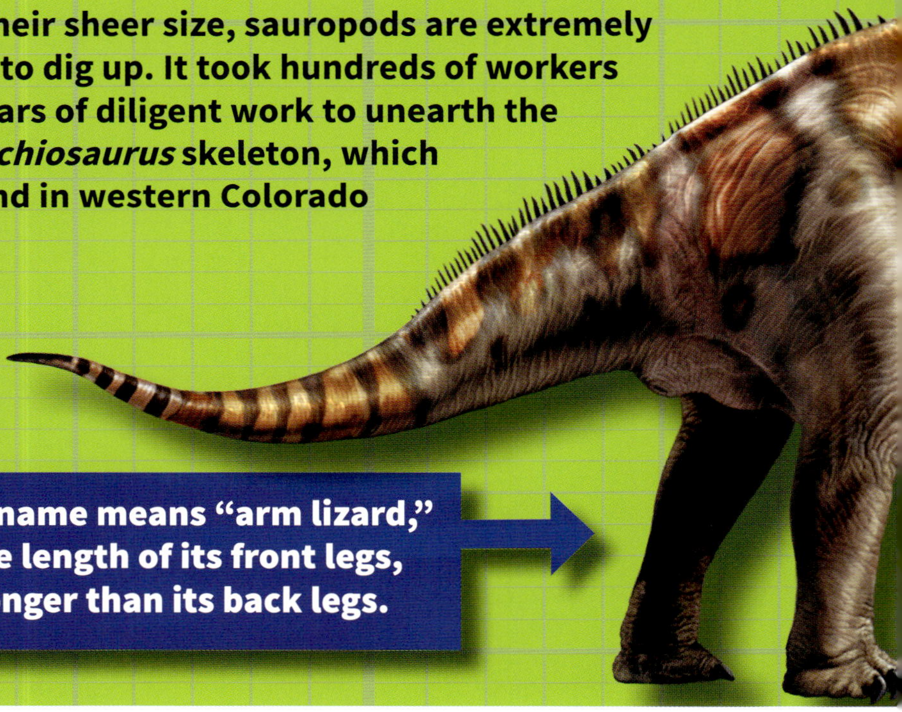

Brachiosaurus's name means "arm lizard," referring to the length of its front legs, which were longer than its back legs.

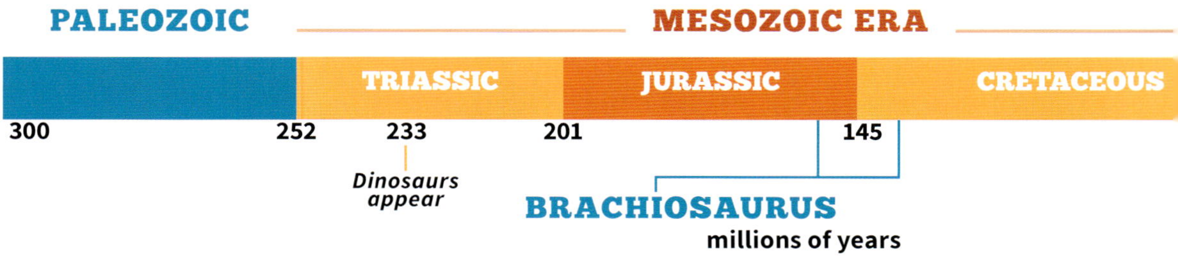

Brachiosaurus

Name Meaning: Arm lizard
Size: 85 feet long; 100,000 pounds
Diet: Plants
Fossils Found In: North America

A long neck allowed *Brachiosaurus* to eat leaves that other dinosaurs couldn't reach.

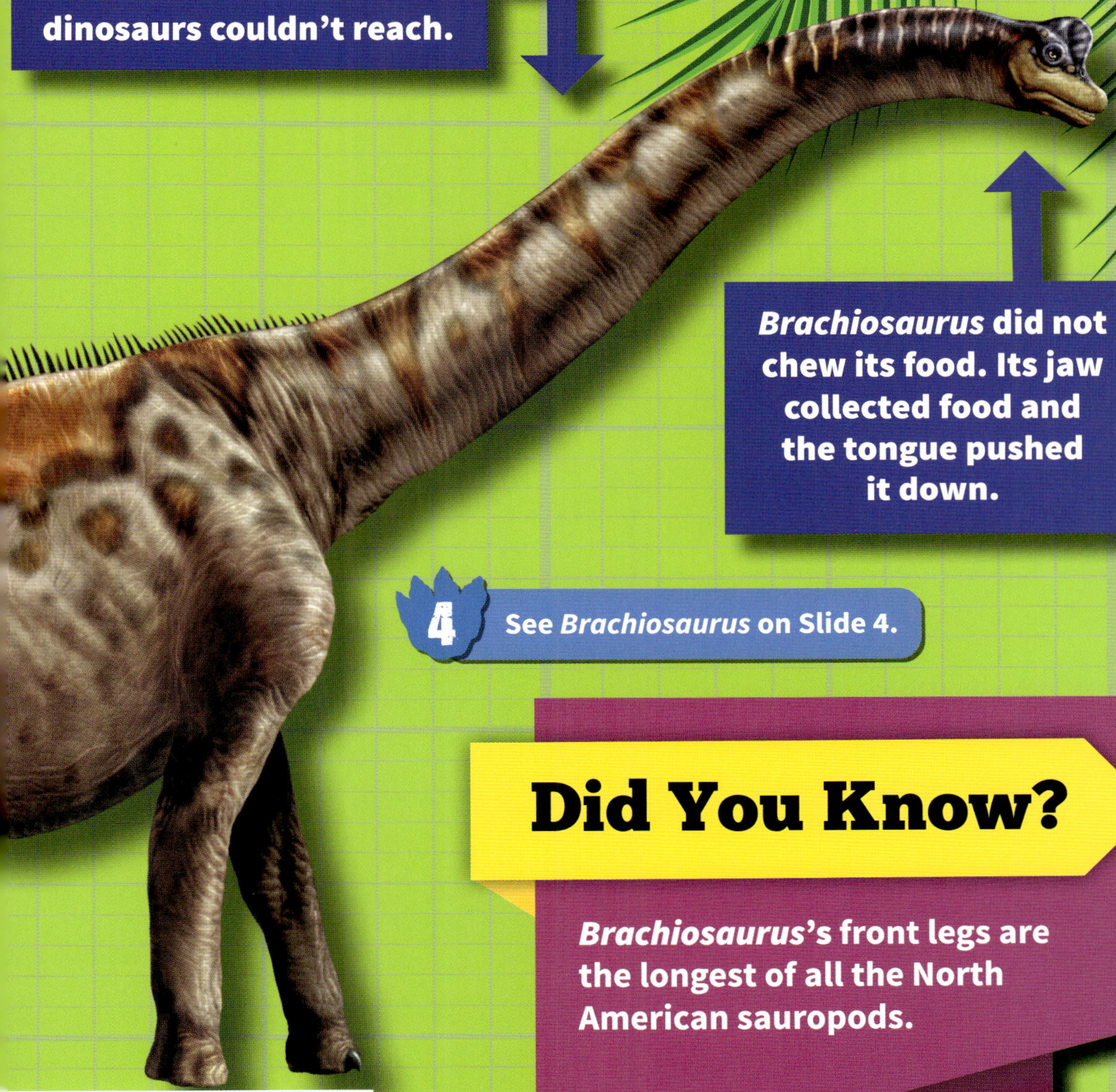

Brachiosaurus did not chew its food. Its jaw collected food and the tongue pushed it down.

4 See *Brachiosaurus* on Slide 4.

Did You Know?

Brachiosaurus's front legs are the longest of all the North American sauropods.

CENOZOIC

66 present

Jurassic Dinosaurs

***Stegosaurus*'s back was covered with plates made from bone. The plates stood up to 2 feet tall and may have been used for protection, mating, or temperature control.**

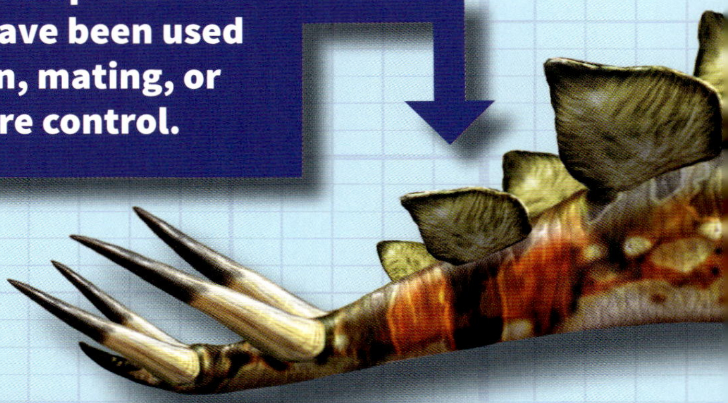

A flexible tail covered in spikes could be whipped to ward off predators.

Stegosaurus

Two rows of bony plates gave *Stegosaurus* its famous profile. These large plates grew from the skin—not the spine. Not sturdy enough to protect against predators, they were probably used to attract mates and frighten rivals.

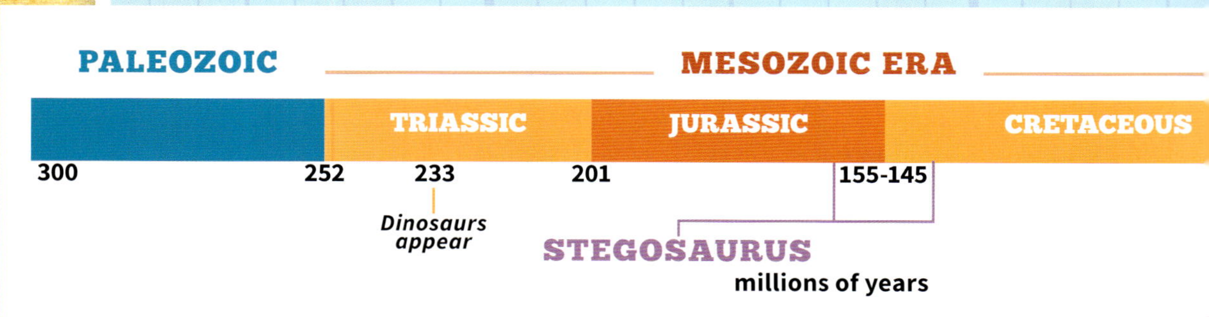

Stegosaurus

Name Meaning: Roofed lizard
Size: 30 feet long; 6,000 pounds
Diet: Plants
Fossils Found In: North America, Europe

DISK 3 1 See *Stegosaurus* on Disk 3, Slide 1.

FAST FACT

Stegosaurus's brain was about the size and shape of a banana.

Stegosaurus could not outrun other dinosaurs. It was a slow walker, only slightly faster than a walking human.

Shorter front legs caused *Stegosaurus*'s head to be low to the ground, so it grazed on short plants such as cycads and conifers.

CENOZOIC

66 present

2 See *Stegosaurus* swinging its tail on Slide 2.

Cretaceous Dinosaurs

A long, thick tail balanced *T. rex*'s enormous body and helped it move quickly.

3 See *T. rex* on Slide 3.

Tyrannosaurus rex

An adult *Tyrannosaurus rex* was bigger than most of today's elephants. But unlike an elephant, it probably had to catch its dinner. Paleontologists now think *T. rex* spent most of its time walking at only 11 miles an hour. Earlier estimates—derived by comparing *T. rex* to an ostrich—were higher, but they didn't take into account the fact that *T. rex* was fifty times heavier.

Young *Tyrannosaurus* probably moved much more quickly. Around the age of thirteen, they had a growth spurt that added almost five pounds a day for four years.

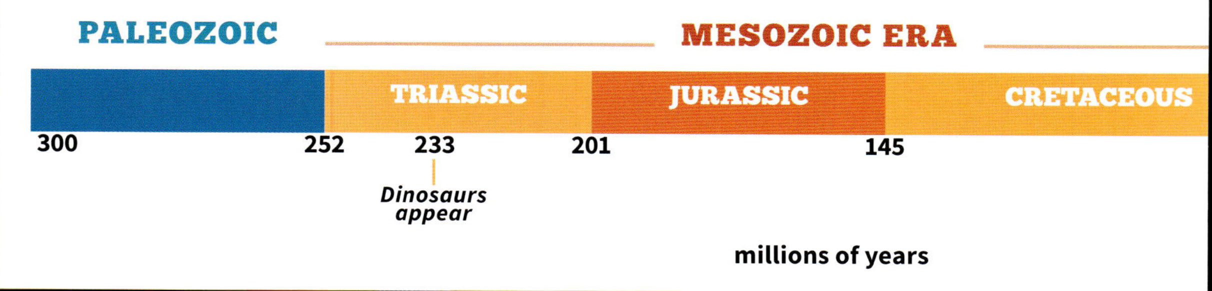

Tyrannosaurus rex

Name Meaning: Tyrant lizard
Size: 40 feet long; 10,000 pounds
Diet: Animals
Fossils Found In: North America

Like birds today, *T. rex* walked on its toes.

Its sharp teeth, up to 12 inches long, were ridged to tear through meat.

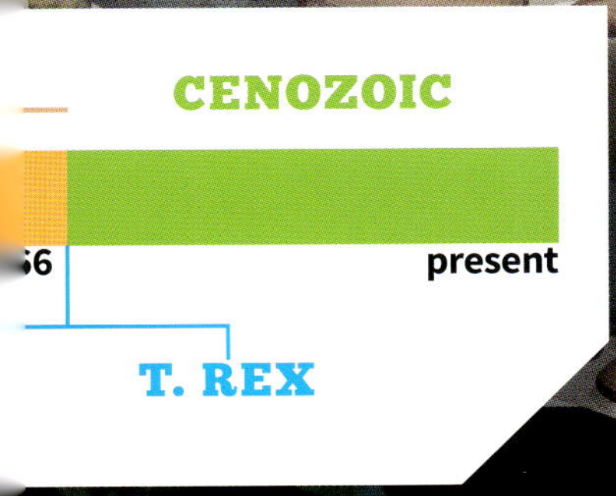

Fantastic Finds

Named for her discoverer, Susan Hendrickson, Sue is the biggest and best-preserved *Tyrannosaurus rex* scientifically described so far. At 90 percent complete, her skeleton reveals evidence of arthritis, parasites, and healed injuries. She was found in South Dakota, but today she can be visited at the Field Museum in Chicago, Illinois.

Cretaceous Dinosaurs

Triceratops

Meat-eating dinosaurs were fearsome killers, so plant-eating dinosaurs needed a way to protect themselves. Some, like *Triceratops*, developed tough skin and horns for protection. *Triceratops* had three sharp horns on its head to defend itself, and a big frill on its neck.

Triceratops had short, strong legs with hooflike toes.

Triceratops

Name Meaning: Three-horned face
Size: 30 feet long; 20,000 pounds
Diet: Plants
Fossils Found In: North America

FAST FACT

Pentaceratops was a ceratopsian, or horned face, dinosaur and a relative of *Triceratops*. Living 5 million years before *Triceratops*, *Pentaceratops* had three horns like *Triceratops,* but its frill was much larger and more ornamented with small spikes.

Pentaceratops's horns were used as weapons and protection against predators. *Pentaceratops* had one of the largest skulls of any ceratopsian. In fact, one *Pentaceratops* skull was discovered that measured almost 8.5 feet long!

4 See *Pentaceratops* on Slide 4.

The frill not only made *Triceratops* look bigger than it really was, but may also have prevented attackers from reaching behind its head to get at its body.

A powerful beak helped *Triceratops* crush through tough plants.

Triceratops's sharp teeth were continuously shed and replaced throughout its life.

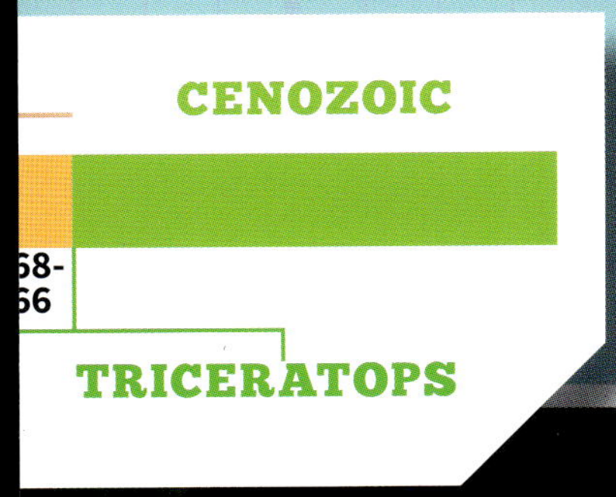

Dinosaur Extinction

Dinosaurs roamed Earth for 165 million years. That's much longer than the 200,000 years that humans have existed. Scientists are constantly uncovering new clues and learning more about the complexity of dinosaurs and their extinction.

Scientists now know that 66 million years ago, a 7-mile wide asteroid crashed into Earth near the Yucatán Peninsula in present-day Mexico. The asteroid impact left a dip in the earth that is 125 miles wide and 12 miles deep. It is called the Chicxulub Crater. The asteroid impact killed off the nonavian dinosaurs and wiped out 75 percent of the plant and animal species on Earth.

DISK 4 1 See the extinction on Disk 4, Slide 1.

2 See an erupting volcano on Slide 2.

For many years, scientists theorized that an increase in volcanic activity in India led to the dinosaurs' extinction. Scientists believed that the volcanoes released sulfur and carbon dioxide into the air, resulting in global warming. Scientists thought the pollutants then settled back to Earth and the temperatures rose abruptly. They believed this shift in the temperature would have been too much for some species to handle. In 2021, scientists studied the amount of carbon dioxide that would have been released from the volcanoes, and the results showed that the volcanoes would not have been the reason for the dinosaurs' extinction.

THE ALVAREZ HYPOTHESIS

In 1980, physicist Luis Walter Alvarez and his son Walter theorized that a 66-million-year-old layer of material called iridium found around Earth was from an asteroid. Iridium, rare in Earth's crust, is a material found in asteroids. In recent years, iridium was also discovered in the asteroid crater itself.

Called the Alvarez hypothesis, this theory was the first to suggest that an asteroid collided with Earth 66 million years ago and caused the dinosaurs' extinction. Though once controversial, today the Alvarez hypothesis is the widely accepted explanation for the extinction of the dinosaurs.

WHAT HAPPENED THE DAY THE ASTEROID HIT?

The collision of the asteroid wreaked havoc on Earth. Debris was thrown into the atmosphere, blocking out the sun. With less sunlight, plants struggled to grow, which affected the animals that ate them. This caused a domino effect, affecting the entire food chain.

Destruction on the planet also occurred by huge tsunamis, powerful earthquakes, and wildfires. The surrounding area around the impact site was destroyed.

3 See an asteroid on Slide 3.

FAST FACT

Fish fossils found in North Dakota suggest that the fish died about an hour after the asteroid impact. When the Chicxulub impact occurred, debris flew into the air and formed glass-like globs called tektites. Scientists know that tektites fell from the sky 15 minutes after the collision. The fish fossils included tektites in the gills, so scientists believe the fish were killed by the collision within an hour's time.

Using computer models, scientists have studied the aftermath of the asteroid. Months after the impact, Earth was plunged into a cold period that many animals couldn't survive. Sulfur from the impact would have combined with rain to create deadly acid rain. Greenhouse gases such as carbon dioxide, methane, and carbon monoxide were released into the atmosphere.

Today, the debris, ash, and toxic material from the asteroid impact is found on Earth in a layer called the K-T boundary. This boundary separates the end of the Cretaceous period from the start of the Tertiary period. Paleontologists have found dinosaur fossils below the K-T layer, but never above it. The K-T boundary is a powerful tool for paleontologists to study to further understand life before, during, and after the extinction.

Scientists believe that the aftereffects of the asteroid would not have killed the dinosaurs instantly. Their extinction would have happened over several decades. Following the end of the Cretaceous, eventually new species of mammals and other life emerged on Earth.

Fossils

Everything we know about dinosaurs we've learned by studying their fossils. Fossils are the remains of animals preserved in the earth. If a living thing dies and happens to be buried in a way that keeps air, scavengers, and bacteria from getting to it, it can become a fossil.

How Fossils Are Formed

To become a fossil, dinosaurs or other prehistoric creatures needed to be covered by sand, mud, or other sediment right after they died. If it gets exposed to the air or elements, the creature will decompose before it can fossilize. As years go by, the dead dinosaur gets buried deeper and deeper under rocky layers of sediment. Minerals from the sediment seep into and replace the dinosaur's bones as the ground around the dinosaur hardens.

Eventually, the minerals and the bones merge together and a rocky copy of the dinosaur is made. As the ground shifts, the fossil gets pushed to the surface to be discovered.

4 See a fossil on Slide 4.

Scientists can date a fossil by examining the rock and other fossils that surround it or by measuring its radioactive decay in uranium or zirconium in the rocks that contain the fossil.

Did You Know?

Bones, shells, and teeth are all familiar fossil types. But tracks, skin impressions, leaf molds, coprolites (fossilized dung), amber (fossilized tree resin), and preserved burrows are fossils too.

DISK 5
1
See dinosaur footprint fossils on Disk 5, Slide 1.

Modern-Day Dinosaurs

Birds are the last living relatives of the dinosaurs of the Mesozoic. In fact, we know that *T. rex*, one of the biggest, scariest beasts that ever walked Earth, is more closely related to birds than it is to any other animal alive today.

Birds descended from a group of dinosaurs called theropods—two-legged dinosaurs. *Velociraptor* was a member of this group.

2 See *Velociraptor* on Slide 2.

Feathers were once believed to have been a unique feature of birds. However, in the 1990s, dinosaur fossils from China were found with feathers!

3 See *Anchiornis* on Slide 3.

Perhaps next time you see a bird, it will inspire you to explore the wonderful world of dinosaurs!

4 See a bird on Slide 4.

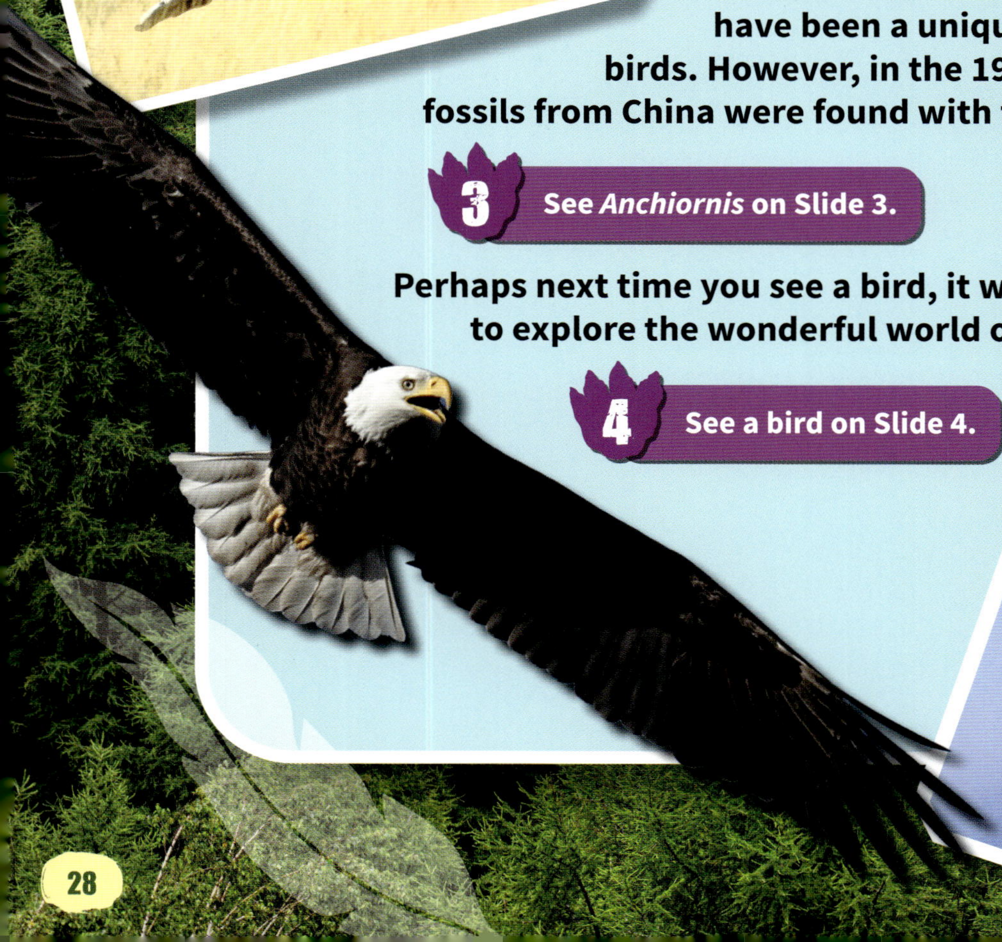